CW00685860

SPIRIT LEVEL

SPIRIT LEVEL
by Pam Valentine

JOSEF WEINBERGER PLAYS

LONDON

Spirit Level
First published in 2015
by Josef Weinberger Ltd
12-14 Mortimer Street, London W1T 3JJ
www.josef-weinberger.com / plays@jwmail.co.uk

Copyright © 2015 by Pam Valentine
Copyright © 2010 by Pam Valentine as an unpublished dramatic composition

The author asserts her moral right to be identified as the author of the work.

ISBN: 978 0 85676 354 0

This play is protected by Copyright. According to Copyright Law, no public
performance or reading of a protected play or part of that play may be given without
prior authorization from Josef Weinberger Plays, as agent for the Copyright Owners.

From time to time it is necessary to restrict or even withdraw the rights of certain
plays. It is therefore essential to check with us before making a commitment to produce
a play.

NO PERFORMANCE MAY BE GIVEN WITHOUT A LICENCE

AMATEUR PRODUCTIONS
Royalties are due at least one calendar month prior to the first performance. A royalty
quotation will be issued upon receipt of the following details:

Name of Licensee
Play Title
Place of Performance
Dates and Number of Performances
Audience Capacity and ticket price(s)

PROFESSIONAL PRODUCTIONS
All enquiries regarding professional rights should be addressed to Josef Weinberger
Plays at the address above. All other enquiries should be made to Film Rights Ltd, 11
Pandora Road, London NW6 1TS

OVERSEAS PRODUCTIONS
Applications for productions overseas should be made to our local authorised agents.
Further information can be found on our website or in our printed Catalogue of Plays.

CONDITIONS OF SALE
This book is sold subject to the condition that it shall not by way of trade or otherwise
be re-sold, hired out, circulated or distributed without prior consent of the Publisher.
**Reproduction of the text either in whole or part and by any means is strictly
forbidden.**

Printed by Short Run Press Ltd, Exeter, Devon UK

Spirit Level was first produced at the Metro Theatre, Vancouver, Canada on 6th November 2010. The cast was as follows:

Jack Cameron	Ryan Johnson
Susie Cameron	Jane E Craven
Mark Webster	Dave McNea
Simon Willis	Robert Medeiros
Felicity Willis	Colleen Lornie
Marcia Bradshaw	Deborah Finkel
Guardian Angel	Tara Webster

Directed and set designed by Don Briard
Costumes designed by Lesley Jack

CHARACTERS

JACK CAMERON

SUSIE CAMERON (his wife)

MARK WEBSTER

SIMON WILLIS

FLIC WILLIS (his wife)

MARCIA BRADSHAW (FLIC's mother)

GUARDIAN ANGEL

SYNOPSIS OF SCENES

ACT ONE

Scene One
The sitting room of Cobbler's Cottage.
A sunny day in June.

Scene Two
The sitting room of Cobbler's Cottage.
Six weeks later.

ACT TWO

Scene One
The sitting room of Cobbler's Cottage.
A sunny day in September.

Scene Two
The sitting room of Cobbler's Cottage.
A few days before Christmas.

Scene Three
The sitting room of Cobbler's Cottage.
Early hours of the morning of the next day.

ACT ONE

Scene One

Time: The Present. A sunny day in June.

The sitting room of Cobbler's Cottage. An attractively but simply furnished room.

An archway right (or door frame with no door: perhaps a pulled back curtain) leads off to right the front door and left the kitchen and stairs. French windows with drawn-back curtains centre back. Backcloth showing terrace, treetops and sky. Two pictures on the wall left. Small tables left and right of the French windows. The table right has a large vase. A desk against the wall left. On the desk an inkstand and a key. Small sofa at an angle right. Small armchair at an angle left. A bookcase against the wall below the door right.

JACK CAMERON is on the sofa, legs stretched out, his hands behind his head, eyes closed. He is in somnolent mood and doesn't want to be disturbed. He is an attractive middle aged man, well dressed in casual clothes. After a moment he sighs deeply and still with his eyes closed folds his arms across his chest.

SUSIE CAMERON enters right. She is slightly younger than JACK. She wears an expensive outfit and has an air of sophistication. She glances at JACK then goes to the French windows and looks out.

SUSIE	Those sweet aquilegias have seeded themselves all over the place. Promiscuous little things, aren't they?
JACK	*(still with his eyes closed)* Mm . . .
SUSIE	The hostas are looking decidedly hung over.

JACK   Mm . . .

SUSIE   Might they need feeding?

JACK   Probably –

SUSIE   Shall I look in the shed and see what there is?

JACK   Why not? . . .

                (*She moves right, has a sudden thought.*)

SUSIE   How will I know if it's the right thing? I
                don't want to kill them.

JACK   If it hasn't got a skull and crossbones on it
                you're in with a chance.

SUSIE   I wish you'd take an interest in the garden.

JACK   There doesn't seem a lot of point, really,
                does there?

SUSIE   Suppose not . . .

                (*She flops into the armchair. Looks round
                the room.*)

SUSIE   I spy with my little –

JACK   Inkstand.

SUSIE   How did you know?

JACK   It's always inkstand.

SUSIE   It is not!

JACK   So how did I know then?

SUSIE   Sorry if I'm boringly predictable.

             (*He remains with his eyes closed. She thinks deeply.*)

             Crusty bread, hunk of Stilton and a pickled onion.

JACK   You haven't spied all that lot, have you?

SUSIE   It's what I'd order if I was having a pub lunch.

JACK   You can't be hungry.

SUSIE   I know I can't but it's what I'd have if I was. What about you?

JACK   (*becoming irritated*) What about me what?

SUSIE   What would you order?

JACK   A foaming pint of bitter.

SUSIE   To eat, what would you order to eat?

JACK   Two foaming pints of bitter.

             (SUSIE *rises and goes to the bookcase right, takes out a book and reads the flyleaf.*)

SUSIE   Oh . . . how sweet! (*She reads.*) 'If this book should chance to roam, box its ears and send it home'. In the dearest little-boy writing. How old were you when you wrote that?

JACK   Forty-two. Susie, I am trying to sleep.

SUSIE   Don't be ridiculous, you know you can't sleep.

JACK   Well, I'm trying. Okay? Go and resuscitate
                the hostas.

                (SUSIE *puts the book back.*)

SUSIE   Under the circumstances I do think you
                could make a bit of an effort to entertain me.

JACK   What would you like? A bouncy castle in the
                garden?

SUSIE   (*going to the French windows*) I have this
                permanent feeling that I'm in quarantine.

JACK   You chose to come here. The world was your
                oyster.

SUSIE   What does that expression mean? It doesn't
                make sense. 'Here's a million pounds.
                Where do you want to go?' 'Oh, please, can
                I go to an oyster?'

JACK   It's metaphorical.

SUSIE   Meta what?

JACK   Metaphorical. A figure of speech. A word
                is transferred from one object to another to
                imply comparison.

SUSIE   So what does an oyster compare with?

JACK   (*opening his eyes and sitting up*) Any bloody
                thing you want it to. Why can women never
                understand that when a man has his eyes
                closed it means he doesn't want to listen to
                endless prattle.

SUSIE   Prattle? Prattle? That's a bit archaic, isn't it?

JACK	I like archaic words, (*He thinks.*) Prattle . . . Shenanigans . . . Bosoms . . .
SUSIE	Bosoms?
JACK	(*quoting*) 'The breast of a human being, especially of a woman'.
SUSIE	I know what they are. Jack, I've got two of them. Standard issue.
	(*She looks through the French windows and sees something.*)
SUSIE	Oh no!
JACK	What?
SUSIE	Look!
	(JACK *goes to the window.*)
JACK	Where?
SUSIE	(*pointing*) In the fruit trees. See?
JACK	Oh . . . this really is too much.
SUSIE	Well, it has been three weeks since –
	(*She listens.*)
	There's someone at the front door.
	(JACK *goes to the doorway right and looks out.*)
JACK	Oh, we are honoured. The boss man himself.
SUSIE	Fun?

JACK

Why not?

(*She takes the key from the desk and puts it under the vase on the table right.* JACK *adjusts the two pictures on the wall so that they are crooked. As they finish* MARK WEBSTER *enters right.* MARK *is middle-aged to elderly, pompous and pedantic. He carries a folder. Ignoring* JACK *and* SUSIE *he looks round the room. His manner is somewhat wary.*)

JACK

(*tugging an imaginary forelock*) Afternoon, Squire!

(SUSIE *moves close to* MARK *and looks at his tie. She points to it.*)

SUSIE

He never went there, did he?

JACK

If he did it was on a day trip.

(MARK *opens the folder and reads.* SUSIE *looks over his shoulder.*)

SUSIE

What a cheek! They've lowered the rent.

JACK

I wish he'd lower his aftershave. He's got enough on to anaesthetise a hip replacement.

(MARK *shuts the folder and looks round the room. Sees the pictures are crooked. Thinks for a moment, then straightens them. Moves to the table right with the vase. Takes a handkerchief from his top pocket and flicks at some dust. He puts the handkerchief away.* SIMON *and* FLIC WILLIS *appear at the French windows. They peer through and rap on the window.* MARK *goes to the window.*)

MARK   *(calling)* Just a moment. I'll get the key and unlock the doors.

          (He goes to the desk. Looks for the key and is obviously puzzled. Goes to the French windows and calls.)

MARK   So sorry, would you mind coming round to the front door?

          (SIMON and FLIC nod and go right. MARK exits right. JACK adjusts the pictures so they are again askew. SUSIE goes to the table right, picks up the vase and takes the key from under it. Is about to replace the vase. Thinks and puts it on the table left. Puts the key on the desk.)

SUSIE   *(fluffing her hair)* How do I look?

JACK   Exquisitely beautiful.

SUSIE   Ah! Thank you, darling.

JACK   Not that anyone's going to see you.

SUSIE   Damn. I keep forgetting.

          (JACK sits on the sofa. SUSIE stands by the bookcase.)

SUSIE   I'm quite pleased, actually. Today's been rather tedious.

JACK   Every day is rather tedious . . .

SUSIE   And whose fault is that?

JACK   Mine, mine, mine, mine, mine. Okay?

SUSIE   Just as long as you know.

                 (*There are voices off.*)

MARK   Shall we make a start in the lounge?

SUSIE   (*with distaste*) Lounge . . . Oh dear . . .

                 (MARK *enters right followed by* SIMON
                 and FLIC. *They are young, eager, and
                 casually dressed but their clothes are more
                 department store than designer.*)

MARK   (*extending hand*) Mark Webster of Webster,
                 Webster and Webster.

JACK   Hooray for nepotism.

SIMON   (*shaking hands*) Simon Willis. This is my
                 wife, Felicity.

FLIC   (*shaking hands*) But everyone calls me Flic.
                 (*She looks round, delighted with the room.*)
                 Oh, this is lovely, isn't it, darling?

SIMON   Wow! (*To* MARK.) You should see some of
                 the old grot we've looked at.

JACK   She's rather sweet, isn't she?

SUSIE   Yes, but she can't see you so stop holding
                 your stomach in.

                 (SIMON *and* FLIC *look round the room.* MARK
                 *looks with them. Looks at the vase left and
                 is puzzled. Looks from one table to the
                 other.*)

FLIC   That desk is beautiful.

MARK   Sorry?

FLIC   That desk. It's beautiful

(MARK *moves towards the desk.*)

MARK   It is, isn't it? In fact quite a few of the pieces are −

(*He sees the key. Picks it up. Stares at it.* SIMON *wanders round and goes to the bookcase.*)

FLIC   It's for six months, isn't it?

MARK   (*looking at the key*) Sorry?

FLIC   The lease. It's for six months?

MARK   Oh, yes . . .

(*Still puzzled, he puts the key on the desk.*)

FLIC   Do you mind? I've got a thing about crooked pictures.

(*She straightens the pictures.*)

That's better.

(MARK *looks from the pictures, to the vase, and then the key. Hesitates, and then decides he has to say something.*)

MARK   There is one thing I must emphasise, should you decide to take the cottage and should anything happen that causes you to leave before the tenancy is up you would be legally liable for the remaining rent.

FLIC   What? Even if the roof falls in?

MARK   I don't mean anything structurally, I mean
             . . . should you move in and then find for
             some reason the property is in any way . . .
             unsuitable. The roof, I assure you is . . .

FLIC   What sort of unsuitable?

JACK   Clanking chains . . .

SUSIE   Low moans . . .

SIMON   Darling! Look –

FLIC   What?

SIMON   The 'Inspector Sharp' books! Every single
             one.

             (FLIC *goes to the bookcase.* SUSIE *stands
             back and watches them.*)

FLIC   (*to* MARK) You'll have to excuse him. He's a
             complete Jack Cameron addict.

             (JACK *beams with pride.* SIMON *takes out a
             book.*)

SUSIE   (*to* JACK) You're wearing that silly grin . . .

             (SUSIE *goes to the French windows.* JACK
             rises and stands next to SIMON.)

SIMON   Look! (*He holds a book.*) 'The Stepney
             Slaughterer'. That's where Inspector Sharp
             matched the cuts on the body to cuts he
             made on a sheep's carcass and proved that
             the knife was the one owned by Todd Baines
             the blind beggar. Brilliant, that was.

JACK   It was rather good.

SIMON   (*with another book*) And 'The Whitechapel
              Warbler'. Oh, that was so clever. You see
              what happened was – people heard this
              funny warbling noise – like a bird – before
              they heard the victim scream, and Inspector
              Sharp realised that the murderer used to
              gargle with port before he –

FLIC   Darling – calm down!

MARK   The thing is – (*He registers* SIMON's *words.*)
              Gargle with port?

SIMON   Yes! Because his mother used to gargle with
              port and he hated his mother because she
              was a prostitute, so he used to gargle with
              port before he strangled his victims and –

FLIC   How could they scream if he was strangling
              them?

JACK   Well spotted.

SIMON   They screamed when they saw his mask.
              The voodoo devil mask from Jakarta.

SUSIE   Is he going to go through the entire plot?

SIMON   Stolen from a witch doctor who was about to
              poison him.

SUSIE   He is, isn't he.

SIMON   But Inspector Sharp heard the dying words
              of his last victim – he bent over her and she
              just managed to say –

FLIC   What about the cottage?

SIMON   (*in a strangled whisper*) Jack – look for the
            man in the – What?

FLIC   We're here to look at the cottage.

JACK   Philistine . . .

SIMON   He's signed it! He has actually signed it!

SUSIE   He's signed them all, darling.

MARK   Well . . . as a matter of fact . . . Cobbler's
            Cottage was owned by Jack Cameron.

SIMON   Oh my God . . . Oh my God. You mean he
            . . . sat in this room . . . looked out of that
            window . . . climbed those stairs . . .

JACK   Shall we stop at the bathroom door?

            (SIMON *collapses onto the sofa.*)

MARK   (*warming to his theme*) This was his country
            retreat – his hideaway – the place where he
            wrote all his books.

SIMON   Wow . . .

FLIC   Did he live alone?

SUSIE   No.

MARK   No, no, he lived here with his wife. Susie, a
            most charming lady . . .

SUSIE   Ah . . .

SIMON   Did you know them?

MARK   Intimately.

JACK   Watch his nose grow.

MARK   Oh yes, I've spent many a happy evening in their company. Dinners . . . parties . . . summer soirées . . .

(He goes to the French windows and looks out. With the air of one who has lost great friends.)

JACK   One dinner when he bored for England, goosed you, and finished my cognac.

MARK   You know how they died, of course.

SIMON   They drowned, didn't they?

MARK   Yes. It was . . . tragic.

FLIC   What happened?

(FLIC and SUSIE both go to sit in the armchair, FLIC gets there first. SUSIE sits on the arm.)

MARK   They were holidaying in the Italian Lakes and apparently they decided to hire a boat and row to the far side of the lake for a picnic. Sadly –

SUSIE   Very sadly, actually.

MARK   – there was some kind of accident. What exactly happened we'll never know. Maybe a sudden squall – maybe one of them leaned over too far –

(He pauses. Enjoying the drama. SIMON and FLIC imagine the happening.)

SUSIE	Or maybe one of them tried to chill the Chianti and fell in.
JACK	And his idiot wife tried to save him and drowned them both.
MARK	That night, when they didn't return for dinner, a search party went out to look for them. The boat was found drifting and their bodies –
SUSIE	I hate this bit.
MARK	Their bodies were washed up some days later.
FLIC	Ugh. Fishes eat bodies, don't they?
JACK / SUSIE	(*bitterly*) Yes.
SIMON	What a waste . . . all that talent . . .
SUSIE	And my Versace dress.
FLIC	But in a way, you know, dying together. It's very romantic,
JACK	Is she mad?
FLIC	(*to* SIMON) I hope something like that happens to us.
SUSIE	Yes, she is.
SIMON	So why hasn't the cottage been sold?
MARK	Ah, well, they had no children –
JACK	Fun trying, though.

(SUSIE *blows him a kiss.*)

MARK   – he was an orphan.

JACK   Don't go into all that.

MARK   She had one niece in . . .

SUSIE   Australia.

MARK   Australia. Who she thinks she might one day come and live here.

JACK   (*in an Aussie accent*) It's a long way from Bondi, Brenda.

MARK   Which is why – for the time being – we're letting it.

FLIC   Is it haunted?

MARK   Haunted? (*He laughs heartily.*) Good heavens, no!

              (SUSIE *goes to the table left puts her hands on the vase and is about to lift it.*)

FLIC   Pity. I would adore to live in a haunted house.

              (SUSIE *removes her hands.*)

SIMON   (*looking directly at* JACK) Jack Cameron sat here. Wow.

MARK   They're hardly likely to erect a blue plaque, but his books were quite popular. I've bought the odd one myself. For a long flight.

JACK   Prick.

SIMON   We've got to live here, darling. Got to.

FLIC   Well, yes, maybe, but I think it would be
             sensible to see the rest of the place first.

MARK   Of course. Would you like to have a
             look upstairs? Marvellous views from
             the bedrooms but the bathroom's a touch
             primitive.

             (*He moves to the door right and stands back
             to let* SIMON *and* FLIC *exit.*)

SUSIE   I suppose his idea of sophistication is an
             avocado bathroom suite and soap on a rope.

             (*She takes the key from the desk and slips
             it into* MARK'S *pocket. He exits right.* SUSIE
             *moves the pictures back to crooked and puts
             the vase on the table, right.*)

             If she likes haunted houses I'm wasting my
             time. But it's fun to watch that pompous
             idiot doubt his own sanity. I suppose we
             could sabotage the plumbing. How are you
             on ballcocks?

             (JACK *isn't listening.*)

             Jack? How do we get rid of them? Supposing
             they –

             (*He looks at her pleadingly.*)

             Oh no. Oh definitely no.

JACK   He likes my books.

SUSIE   Don't be so pathetic.

JACK   Couldn't we give them a try?

SUSIE   Remember the last couple we gave a try?

JACK   I didn't know he played the bugle.

SUSIE   We'll have no peace. No cosy evenings. No
            privacy

JACK   They'll be out all day –

SUSIE   You don't know that,

JACK   Of course they will. That's what couples do
            now. Get up at the crack of dawn – flog to
            the station – eight hours in a stuffy office –
            quick slurp in a wine bar – then the whole
            procedure in reverse. Back here at eight,
            quick gin and frozen dinner then bed. Forget
            sex.

SUSIE   I have.

JACK   Sunday morning if there's a strong head
            wind.

SUSIE   Thank you very much!

JACK   What?

SUSIE   I didn't know it took a strong head wind
            before you claimed your conjugals.

JACK   Claimed my – now whose using archaic
            language?

SUSIE   It's an archaic occupation.

JACK   And we didn't just do it on Sunday
                    mornings.

SUSIE   No. Sometimes it was Sunday afternoon.
                    After you woke up and before 'Songs of
                    Praise.'

JACK   Susie, Susie, is there much point now in
                    having a row about our defunct sex life?

SUSIE   Defunct?

JACK   That's what we are. Defunct.

SUSIE   We are not defunct. We're dead. That's
                    completely different,

JACK   It means the same thing, woman! Defunct –
                    dead. Dead – defunct.

SUSIE   Stop it. Dead . . . me. If I could cry, I'd cry.

JACK   Of course you can cry.

SUSIE   You can't sleep.

JACK   Whoever heard of the sleeping ghost? But
                    crying – that's completely different. The
                    Weeping Woman of Wilmington? The
                    Sobbing Spectre of . . . Sidcup.

SUSIE   Those are proper ghosts.

JACK   My darling girl, we are proper ghosts.

SUSIE   (*bitterly*) Thanks to you. Only you would get
                    right up to the pearly gates, tell Saint Peter
                    you're an atheist, and get sent down again.

JACK   (*nobly*) I was being truthful.

SUSIE   Why? You never were when you were alive.
               And I get sent down with you.

JACK   Oh no, I'm not having that. He said – you
               know he did – 'She can stay.' And what sort
               of talk is that from a saint? 'She can stay.'
               Pearly Gates . . . there wasn't a pearl in
               sight.

SUSIE   And the Blue Danube isn't blue and the Red
               Sea isn't red.

JACK   And there were 'keep off the grass' signs.

SUSIE   Of course there were! Remember the
               queues? You can't have hoards of wannabe
               angels tramping over your manicured lawns.
               It was probably completely different inside.

JACK   If there is an inside.

SUSIE   Jack! He described it to you. It sounded
               wonderful.

JACK   Exactly. All that hard sell.

SUSIE   Hard sell? You were talking to Saint Peter!

JACK   Was I? For all we know he was some
               heavenly time share tout. Get you inside and
               won't let you out till you've bought a cloud.

SUSIE   Paradise. Gateway to paradise. Saint Peter.
               And you still won't believe in God.

JACK   And with very good reason. Who do you
               know who has ever had a prayer granted?
               Come on, who?

SUSIE   What a selfish attitude, 'I'll only believe in
               you if you answer my prayers.'

JACK   Try before you buy. What's wrong with that?

SUSIE   Perhaps some prayers aren't meant to be
               answered.

JACK   How convenient. Heads you lose, tails you
               lose!

               (*There are voices off.*)

SUSIE   They're coming down.

JACK   (*pleadingly*) Please?

SUSIE   (*firmly*) No.

               (SIMON *and* FLIC *enter right.*)

SIMON   Spooky!

FLIC   Do you think so?

SIMON   Well, definitely weird. He doesn't seem to
               be listening to anything we say.

FLIC   Oh! I thought you meant the cottage was
               spooky.

SUSIE   So did I.

SIMON   No, I love the cottage.

SUSIE   Damn.

SIMON   Jack Cameron lived here . . . wow.

SUSIE   He'll say 'wow' all the time . . .

FLIC　　　　Can we afford it?

SIMON　　　No. Unless he comes down a bit on the rent.

　　　　　　(MARK *enters right*.)

MARK　　　Would you like a wander round the –

　　　　　　(*He sees the vase has moved. Stares at it.*)

FLIC　　　　There isn't a subsidence problem, is there?

MARK　　　Subsidence?

　　　　　　(*He looks from* FLIC *to the vase then to* FLIC.)

FLIC　　　　Those pictures are crooked again.

　　　　　　(MARK *looks. Is shaken but brazens it out.*)

MARK　　　Ah . . . That's because – because – in old
　　　　　　cottages footsteps upstairs disturb the
　　　　　　floorboards and that – that causes a tremor
　　　　　　and . . . and that's why at night you might
　　　　　　hear odd noises.

FLIC　　　　Noises?

MARK　　　Just creaks and . . . creaks and . . . general
　　　　　　sounds of . . . creaking. From the beams.

　　　　　　(JACK, SUSIE, SIMON *and* FLIC *look up.*)

SIMON　　　What beams?

MARK　　　Er . . . roof beams. And sometimes things
　　　　　　slightly –

　　　　　　(*He picks up the inkstand.*)

MARK   – move.

              (*He puts the inkstand down. Looks at the
              desk. Looks again.*)

              How very odd . . . I thought I put the key
              back.

FLIC   Perhaps it's in your pocket?

MARK   (*feeling in his pocket*) No, I wouldn't have
              done that because –

              (*He produces the key. Stares at it.* SIMON
              and FLIC *look at each other.* SIMON *makes a
              hand movement to suggest* MARK *is loopy.*
              SUSIE *pushes the inkstand to the other end of
              the desk.*)

FLIC   Is that why the other couple left? Because of
              the creaks?

MARK   (*nervously*) Other couple?

FLIC   Yes, when we rang, your receptionist said
              we were in luck because the other couple
              left suddenly. Why was that?

JACK   I put bubble bath in his bugle.

MARK   (*thinking swiftly*) Ah yes, unfortunately his
              Company moved him to . . . Moscow.

FLIC   Moscow?

MARK   Moscow. He was . . . (*Searching for
              inspiration.*) in the fur trade.

SIMON   Surely there is no fur trade now?

MARK   (*relieved*) Exactly. That's why they moved
              him to Moscow. (*Swiftly changing the subject.*)
              Err . . . I have no wish to pressurise you but
              there are other people wanting to view . . .

JACK   Oh, don't fall for that old line.

              (FLIC *nudges* SIMON, *reminding him about
              the rent.*)

SIMON   Err . . . we do like it but . . . the thing is . . .

MARK   Yes?

SIMON   We wondered if . . . if you could . . . if you
              could possibly . . .

MARK   Yes?

SIMON   If you could possibly . . .

FLIC   Come down a bit on the rent.

MARK   We have already come – considered coming
              down on the rent. But for a desirable letting
              such as this . . .

FLIC   Suppose we signed for a year?

MARK   (*sucking in his breath*) Mm . . .

JACK   Go on, you mean old bugger. Let 'em have
              it!

SUSIE   I'm warning you! If he says yes it's me for
              the pearly gates.

MARK   Well, for a year's tenancy . . . what about . . .
              less twenty-five a month?

FLIC   What about fifty a month?

MARK   Fifty! Oh . . . I really don't think we could –

                (*He puts the key on the desk. Sees the
                inkstand has moved. Looks from one end of
                the desk to the other.* SIMON *and* FLIC *look at
                each other.*)

SIMON   Mr Webster?

MARK   What?

SIMON   Could you come down?

MARK   Come down?

                (*He looks at the inkstand.*)

SUSIE   I shot myself in the foot with that inkstand,
                didn't I . . .

MARK   Very well. But I do stress that should
                anything happen and you decide not to stay
                you would be liable for –

                (FLIC *sways.* SIMON *rushes to her.*)

SUSIE   Jack! Get some water!

                (JACK *exits right.*)

SIMON   Oh, darling, quick, sit down.

                (*He sits her on the sofa.*)

MARK   Is it the heat?

SIMON   Probably. And she didn't have any lunch.

MARK   I'll get some water.

                (MARK *exits right.* SIMON *sits next to* FLIC,
                one arm round her, one hand on the arm of
                the sofa.)

FLIC   Oh, I'm so sorry . . .

SIMON   Don't be silly.

                (JACK *enters right with a glass of water.*
                He puts the glass in SIMON's *hand. Without*
                looking SIMON *takes it and holds it to* FLIC's
                mouth.)

SIMON   (*he thinks to* MARK) Thanks. (*To* FLIC.) This
                is my fault. Too much tramping around on a
                hot day.

SUSIE   I fainted in Rome, remember? When I
                bought that bracelet.

JACK   So did I when I saw the price.

                (FLIC *waves the glass away. Without looking*
                SIMON *hands the glass to* JACK.)

SIMON   Thanks, that seems to have done the trick.

                (JACK *takes it and is crossing the room to*
                put in on the desk as MARK *enters right*
                with a glass of water. He sees the first glass
                travelling across the room and landing on
                the desk.)

SUSIE   Look at his face! If he wasn't an estate agent
                I could almost feel sorry for him.

JACK   But he is, so don't.

FLIC   I'm fine now. Really.

              (*She sits up and smiles.*)

              Sorry about that. The thing is –

SIMON   (*swiftly cutting in*) Let's go back to Mr
              Webster's office and sort out the business
              side.

MARK   (*still dazed*) What? Oh . . . (*Fervently.*) Yes.
              Let's go back to my office. I'll . . . I'll wait
              for you outside.

              (*He looks nervously round the room. Exits
              right.*)

SIMON   Sure you're okay?

FLIC   Normal service is resumed.

SIMON   You were brilliant over the money.

FLIC   I was, wasn't I? (*She thinks.*) Why did he
              keep on about 'should anything happen?'

SIMON   Maybe they're planning a motorway at the
              end of the garden.

JACK   They were. I bribed the council.

FLIC   Oh well, it's a big garden.

SIMON   I can't believe it. Jack Cameron's cottage . . .

SUSIE   How do I do low moans?

              (*She makes some gurgling noises.*)

              No, that's not it . . .

FLIC	Should we have told him?
SIMON	What? Oh, we will when we've signed the lease. There might be a clause saying no babies.
SUSIE	(*stopping in mid gurgle*) A baby! Oh, wonderful!
JACK	A baby . . . Oh, hell!
FLIC	Where will you work?
SIMON	(*going to the desk*) Here. Where the great man worked.
JACK	(*alarm bells ringing*) What?
SIMON	Who knows? Maybe he'll inspire me.
JACK	No, please no . . .
SUSIE	Please no what?
FLIC	And maybe one day we'll have a bookcase full of your books.
SUSIE	(*understanding*) Oh . . .
	(SIMON *holds out a hand to* FLIC.)
SIMON	Come on, let's go and do the business.
	(FLIC *takes his hand and rises.*)
JACK	I'm not having this. I'm not!
	(JACK *goes to the table right and is about to pick up the vase.* SUSIE *holds it down. They struggle.*)

SUSIE   No! You'll terrify her!

JACK   Good!

FLIC   (*sighing in contentment*) It's so peaceful . . .

SUSIE   (*shouting*) You wanted them here!

SIMON   It is, isn't it?

JACK   (*shouting*) I didn't know he was a writer and she was pregnant!

FLIC   I can hear the birds singing.

SUSIE   (*shouting*) If you smash that vase I'll kill you!

FLIC   The pram can go on the terrace.

JACK   Screaming, squalling, coochie coos all over the place.

SIMON   We'll have to fix up a baby alarm.

JACK   The hell you will.

               (JACK *wins the vase. Lifts it high.*)

FLIC   Goodbye, little cottage. I'll see you soon. Don't worry. You won't be lonely for much longer. I'm going to dust you and polish you and love you like you should be loved.

SIMON   It can't hear you.

FLIC   Yes, it can.

(JACK *holds the vase aloft.* FLIC *blows a kiss to the room.* JACK *lowers the vase.* FLIC *and* SIMON *exit right.*)

JACK   I already know I am going to regret doing that . . .

(*Curtain.*)

Scene Two

The sitting room at Cobbler's Cottage. A few weeks later. The French windows are open. On the bookcase right a tray with drinks and glasses. The room is untidy. Coffee mugs on the floor and the desk. Newspapers strewn over the sofa. JACK *is looking over the shoulder of* SIMON *who is at the desk pecking at his laptop. Sheets of paper on the floor next to a printer.* JACK *shakes his head, goes to the sofa, sits, picks up a newspaper. He opens it and reads.* SUSIE *enters right.*

SUSIE   How's Jean Paul Sartre doing?

JACK   A plot would help.

SUSIE   Be fair, he's just . . . walking round the edges.

JACK   Yes, of a big black hole. (*Putting the paper down.*) It's always the same. Everyone thinks they can write a book. Remember all those parties? (*He imitates a slightly tipsy partygoer.*) 'Oh, I've often thought I could write.' But can they? No. And why can't they? Because they will not work at it.

            (SIMON *rises, yawns. Scratches his head, scratches under one arm, then scratches his crotch.*)

SUSIE   And in a few years' time he'll do all that in
               front of his wife.

               (SIMON *exits through the French windows.*
               JACK *sniffs the air.*)

JACK   Are you wearing perfume?

SUSIE   Miss Dior.

JACK   Where did you – Susie! I thought we agreed
               their bedroom was strictly off limits.

SUSIE   Our bedroom. I was looking for something
               to wear.

JACK   You can't wear Flic's clothes!

SUSIE   A touch young, do you think?

JACK   Yes, but that's not the point. You'll be a
               dress with no one in it. Terrifying sight.

               (*He picks up the newspaper and reads.*)

SUSIE   It's too bad. I'm given one minute to choose
               an outfit that I now have to wear for all
               eternity. If Saint Peter was Saint Petronella
               I'd have been allowed to pack a suitcase.

JACK   Good Lord! Charlie Ribblestock's died. I
               was at school with him.

SUSIE   Well, if we went to heaven you'd have
               someone to talk to.

JACK   Shout to. The man had terminal BO.

               (*He carries on reading.*)

SUSIE	Are there boutiques in heaven, do you suppose?
JACK	Find out. You've got a return ticket.
SUSIE	I'm not going back without you. Who would I talk to?
JACK	Charlie Ribblestock, but stay downwind.
SUSIE	What kind of an existence is this? Can't eat, can't drink, can't sleep, stuck in the same outfit all the time.
JACK	I think it's called the afterlife. And if you hadn't tried to rescue me we wouldn't be in it.
SUSIE	Thanks very much! What was I supposed to do? Let you drown?
JACK	Susie, I did drown.
SUSIE	Yes, but look on the bright side – I drowned with you. Think how awful it would be if I was here and you were here and I didn't know you were here.

(*He looks at her.*)

	You know what I mean. Imagine watching me grieve for you? Weeks of agony . . .
JACK	Weeks?
SUSIE	Months then. Don't nit-pick.

(*She picks up a paper from the desk and reads.*)

SUSIE   Oh, I see what you mean . . .

JACK   (*still reading the obituary*) 'He never
             married.' Comes as no surprise. He was in
             my dormitory . . .

SUSIE   Could you help him?

JACK   Huh! I said no then and I'd say no now.

SUSIE   Simon! With the book. Couldn't you help
             him?

             (JACK *puts the paper down.*)

JACK   What? Be his ghost writer?

SUSIE   There's a baby coming and they're
             overdrawn and –

JACK   No one helped me. If he thinks he can write
             a book let him – how do you know they're
             overdrawn?

SUSIE   What? Oh, err, the bank statement was on
             the table in the kitchen.

JACK   Your eyelid twitches when you tell a lie.

             (FLIC *enters right. She surveys the room and
             is not pleased.*)

FLIC   Simon! Where are you? (*She goes to the
             French windows and calls.*) Simon!

JACK   (*rising*) Why is she in such a bad mood?

SUSIE   I don't know . . . She hasn't felt sick for ages
             . . . can't be that.

(SIMON *enters through the French windows.*)

FLIC   Look at this room!

(JACK, SUSIE *and* SIMON *look round the room.*)

You know my mother's coming.

JACK   I didn't know that!

SUSIE   Neither did I. You'd think she'd have said.

SIMON   Oh God . . . The ice cold cheek then, 'Any
              sign of regular employment, Simon? No, I
              meant paid employment, Simon.'

FLIC   Thank your lucky stars she's not staying.
              She wanted to.

SIMON   No, Please, no!

FLIC   Don't worry. She changed her mind when
              she heard there was only one bathroom.

(*She exits right.*)

SIMON   Thank you, Jack Cameron, for never having
              another bathroom put in. Because I would
              rather be dragged naked over broken
              glass and dropped into a tank of piranhas
              than work at that desk with the Beast of
              Basingstoke breathing down my neck.

JACK   Why doesn't he write like that?

(FLIC *enters right with a tray and gathers up
the mugs.*)

FLIC   You're very unfair to Mummy, you know.

JACK   Is he? No income, a baby coming, I'm on her
            side.

SIMON   Am I? Our wedding? Dressed in black
            from head to toe and wept – no, sobbed –
            throughout the service.

SUSIE   All women cry at weddings. It's tradition.

FLIC   She was missing Daddy.

SIMON   She was wishing you'd married that nerd
            with the Porsche.

FLIC   Ferrari, and William is not a nerd.

SIMON   Any man who sniffs the wine cork is a nerd.
            She thinks – and makes it perfectly obvious
            – that I am not and never will be good
            enough for you.

JACK   I wouldn't argue with that . . .

SIMON   But for your sake I will be polite.

FLIC   Thank you.

SIMON   For as long as I can.

            (*He kisses her.*)

            You smell nice.

FLIC   Miss Dior. Oh, that reminds me, have you
            been moving things around on my dressing
            table?

            (JACK *looks at* SUSIE.)

SIMON   Yes, I was looking for the nail scissors.

(Susie *looks at* Jack.)

FLIC   And did you get the bank statements out of
               the drawer?

SIMON   Probably.

FLIC   And did you put my blue dress on the –

SIMON   Flic, Flic, listen to me –

               (*He takes the tray puts it down and holds
               her hands.*)

               – the only people who live here are us. Okay?

FLIC   What do you mean?

SIMON   You know what I mean.

FLIC   It's just that sometimes I feel . . .

SIMON   You don't feel anything. You *hope* that Jack
               and what's-her-name Cameron are floating
               around watching us. Which I find very
               spooky and will you please stop.

               (Jack *and* Susie *stand either side of them.*)

FLIC   Susie. Her name is Susie, (*Pause.*) Do you
               think they're happy?

SIMON   I don't know? You were the one who went
               to Sunday school. What did they hand out
               about heaven?

FLIC   Perfect happiness.

SIMON   They're you go then. They're perfectly happy.

FLIC   But supposing they're not. Supposing
               they're wishing they were here, in their
               lovely cottage, and what if they –

SIMON   Flic, listen to me. Only cranks and
               nutters believe in ghosts and spooks and
               apparitions. The Loch Ness Monster is dead
               in the water and the Tooth Fairy doesn't
               exist. Okay?

FLIC   What about Father Christmas?

SIMON   He's real.

FLIC   That's all right, then.

               (*She exits right with the tray.* SIMON *kneels
               down and picks up papers.* SUSIE *tidies the
               papers on the desk.*)

JACK   What are you doing?

SUSIE   Helping.

JACK   You're a ghost, not an au pair. Leave things
               alone

SUSIE   He won't notice.

               (SUSIE *puts the paper back in a pile.*
               SIMON *gets up and puts his papers in the
               wastepaper basket. Then looks at the desk.*
               FLIC *enters right and picks up newspapers
               from the sofa. She sees* SIMON *staring at the
               desk.*)

FLIC   What's the matter?

SIMON   I thought – (*Hastily.*) – Nothing, nothing.

(With a puzzled look at the desk he picks up the laptop.)

FLIC   What are you doing?

SIMON   Putting it in the summerhouse. In the faint hope that if your mother can't see the laptop she won't ask about the book.

              (SIMON exits through the French windows.)

FLIC   She will . . .

              (She exits right with the newspapers.)

SUSIE   We'll have to be careful. I don't want Flic thinking the place is haunted . . .

JACK   I love the 'we'. And she's longing for it to be haunted.

SUSIE   She thinks she is, but it might upset her. And I want this to be the perfect pregnancy.

JACK   Hoping to be Godmother, are we?

SUSIE   Oh! Wouldn't that be wonderful?

JACK   Susie – we are dead – dead people cannot stand at the font and promise to denounce the Devil and all his works.

SUSIE   Guardian angel then. Hey! I wonder if I've got one?

              (She looks round.)

              Hello? Hello-o? Guardian Angel, can you hear me?

(She listens.)

JACK   What are you hoping for? A rush of wings?

SUSIE   Of course not. Saint Peter didn't have wings.

JACK   No, he had a rather nice Rolex watch,
              though.

SUSIE   Well, he can hardly check people in with a
              sundial, can he? (*She calls in a sing song
              voice.*) Guardian Angel? Can you hear me?

              *(She listens. JACK shakes his head at her
              innocence. Suddenly a woman appears
              in the French windows. She is dressed in
              black. Wearing a hat with a half veil.)*

SUSIE   That was quick! (*She regards the woman.*)
              She's not a bit what I expected . . .

              (The woman enters. SUSIE goes to her.)

              How do you do? Err . . . very nice of you to
              come so quickly. (*She hesitates a moment.*)
              Forgive me, but – has someone died?

              (The woman ignores SUSIE.)

              (In the woman's ear.) Hello!

              *(The woman is MARCIA BRADSHAW, FLIC'S
              mother. A difficult and forbidding woman
              and a terrible snob. Lifting her veil, she
              surveys the room and makes a tutting noise.)*

JACK   That's not your Guardian Angel. It's the
              Beast of Basingstoke.

MARCIA   Dear, dear, dear . . .

SUSIE   I hate her.

JACK   Give the woman a chance –

MARCIA   No room to swing a cat . . .

JACK   So do I.

     (FLIC *enters right.*)

FLIC   Mummy!

MARCIA   Felicity, darling!

     (*She embraces* FLIC.)

     Let me look at you.

     (*She steps back and studies* FLIC.)

     You're very peaky.

SUSIE   Just what a girl wants to hear.

FLIC   Did you ring the bell?

MARCIA   No, dear. I thought you might be resting.

FLIC   Resting?

MARCIA   When I was expecting you, Daddy insisted that I spent from three till four with my legs raised.

JACK   Ghastly thought.

FLIC   I don't need to rest. I'm not looking peaky. I'm fine, (*She looks round.*) What do you think? It's sweet, isn't it?

MARCIA   (*unimpressed*) It's certainly bijou . . .

FLIC   Oh Mummy! Once upon a time ten people
                would have lived here.

MARCIA   Very probably, dear, but they were peasants.

SUSIE   You old cow.

                (MARCIA *goes to a spot near* SUSIE *and sniffs.*)

FLIC   What is it?

MARCIA   Are you septic tank or main drainage?

SUSIE   Just dead, love.

FLIC   I've no idea . . .

MARCIA   Probably septic tank. That could be the
                cause.

FLIC   Cause of what?

MARCIA   The smell.

JACK   This from a woman who's been rolling in
                mothballs.

MARCIA   Faint, but it's there. Have you had it
                surveyed?

FLIC   We're renting it, not buying it.

MARCIA   Renting . . . My daughter. Renting. It breaks
                my heart.

                (*She sits in the armchair.*)

JACK   What heart?

MARCIA   Come home. You know your room is always
                there waiting for you.

FLIC   (*amused*) What about Simon?

MARCIA   (*dismissively*) Oh, him too I suppose. Please
                do. Felicity. It's a very lonely house without
                you. And Daddy.

                (*She takes a hankie and dabs her eyes.* SUSIE
                pretends to be sick. FLIC *goes to* MARCIA *and
                sits on the arm of the chair.*)

FLIC   Oh, please, Mummy.

SUSIE   Yes. Please, Mummy.

FLIC   It has been three years. (*She hesitates.*)
                Don't you think after all this time you
                should be . . . moving on?

MARCIA   Moving on? How can I possibly move on?
                He's always with me. He's here now.

                (JACK *and* SUSIE *look round.*)

                Sometimes I think I can hear him talking to
                me.

JACK   Come on, Daddy, now's your chance.

MARCIA   Thirty years . . .

JACK   With her? Poor sod,

                (SIMON *enters through the French windows.
                Sees* MARCIA. *Braces himself.*)

SIMON   Marcia.

MARCIA	(*offering a cheek which he gingerly kisses*) Simon. Are you well?
SIMON	Very well, thank you.
MARCIA	Any sign of regular –
FLIC	(*swiftly*) Isn't it exciting that a famous author once lived here?
MARCIA	Yes . . . Odd that he chose to live in such humble surroundings.
SUSIE	Tell her about the London flat! Tell her!
SIMON	This was his country hideaway.
MARCIA	Hideaway is right. Impossible to find and then that rutted cart track.
JACK	To keep people like you away, love.
MARCIA	And you say they drowned?
FLIC	Yes, so sad.
MARCIA	What I don't understand is how they could be so foolish as to go out in a boat without taking full safety precautions.
SUSIE	We didn't know the Italian for life jacket.
MARCIA	So tell me, Simon –
FLIC	(*swiftly*) Why don't I go and make the tea?
SIMON	Or would you rather have a drink?
MARCIA	It's a little early for me, but please – if you feel the need.

SIMON	I didn't. But I do now.
	(*He goes to the drinks tray.* MARCIA *gives him a chilling look.*)
SIMON	(*holding up a bottle*) Flic?
MARCIA	Felicity is pregnant.
SIMON	I know. I was there when it happened.
FLIC	(*eager to change the mood*) How's the garden, Mummy?
MARCIA	Missing Daddy dreadfully.
SIMON	(*raising his glass and drinking*) Cheers!
JACK	Boy's got guts . . .
FLIC	Is old Ben still helping you?
MARCIA	When sober. I think I would like some tea, dear.
FLIC	Oh, right. I'll . . . I'll just put the kettle on.
	(*She moves right and gives an anxious look back.* SIMON *and* MARCIA *smile sweetly at her. She exits right.*)
MARCIA	So tell me, Simon, what news on the job front? Any sign of regular employment?
SIMON	I have regular employment, Marcia. You know that.
MARCIA	I meant paid employment.
SIMON	Ah. Well, I've applied for a paper round.

MARCIA   Really! You stand there, glass in hand –

SIMON   Empty glass!

                (*He goes to the drinks and refills his glass.*)

MARCIA   I'm amazed you can even afford cooking
                sherry. No income. Felicity to support, a
                baby coming – I find the whole situation
                very worrying.

SIMON   Slightly worrying. But once I sell my book –

MARCIA   Pie in the sky. Daddy used to say everyone
                has a book in them. Six of them will write it
                and one of them see it published.

JACK   You're right there, Daddy.

SIMON   Then let's hope I'm that one. And we have
                planned for this year so there's no need to –

MARCIA   I'd better give Felicity some money.

SIMON   No, thank you.

JACK   Take it, you fool!

SIMON   Once my book sells –

MARCIA   How is it progressing? This 'Book'?

SIMON   Brilliantly.

                (JACK *looks at him with raised eyebrows.*)

MARCIA   Daddy used to say that supreme confidence
                is either a sign of great ability or great
                stupidity.

SIMON	Did he? Well, good for Daddy. Marcia – shall we once and for all –

(FLIC *enters right.*)

FLIC	I thought you'd prefer tea in the dining room, Mummy.
MARCIA	Lovely, dear. But I think Simon was about to say something?
SIMON	(*with great meaning*) It can wait.
MARCIA	(*rising*) Oh, before I forget. William sends his love. He came to see me before he went to Antigua. Still not married . . .

(MARCIA *and* FLIC *exit right.* SIMON *puts his hands into a throttling position and follows them.*)

SUSIE	Bitch. Copper-bottomed bitch. What are we going to do and don't say nothing.
JACK	I wasn't going to and I don't know . . .

(*He sits in the armchair.*)

Oh God – it's still warm.

SUSIE	Septic tank indeed. You've got to help him.
JACK	Now I've met the black widow there's nothing I'd like better. How on earth did she produce that lovely girl?

(SUSIE *sits on the sofa.*)

SUSIE	Daddy helped.

JACK   Daddy would have needed help. I bet she
              only let him do it when there was an R in
              the month.

SUSIE   We must do something.

JACK   Yes, but what?

SUSIE   Suppose you . . . wrote a plot and hid it
              somewhere and led him to it?

JACK   What with? Breadcrumbs?

SUSIE   Perhaps if you . . . What if you . . .
              Supposing you . . .

              (*They go into deep thought.* JACK *rests his
              head in his hands.* SUSIE *leans her head
              back, closes her eyes, and furrows her brow.
              A woman appears in the French windows.
              She holds her hat on her head and skids
              to a halt as if propelled by a strong wind.
              Middle-aged, dressed in tweedy old clothes,
              carrying a capacious bag. Looking as
              though she might be collecting for a charity.
              She leans against the French windows,
              straightens her spectacles. She is* SUSIE'S
              GUARDIAN ANGEL. *She sighs deeply.* JACK
              and SUSIE *look up. Startled. She takes her
              spectacles off and polishes them on her
              petticoat.*)

JACK   We needn't have bothered to have a front
              door.

SUSIE   She must be collecting for something.

JACK   Whatever it is she should have knocked.
              Damn cheek, walking straight in.

(*The* ANGEL *puts her spectacles on and smiles at them.*)

ANGEL   That's better. Which of you called me out?

SUSIE   (*astounded*) Can you . . . see us?

ANGEL   Of course I can. (*She gives* JACK *a piercing look.*) Only too clearly.

            (*Susie remembers her earlier call to her Guardian Angel.*)

SUSIE   Oh! Are you my Guardian Angel?

ANGEL   It was you, was it? Sorry about the delay but since the cutbacks the old days of one to one are over and I was in the middle of a case conference when you called. What a nice outfit. Silly me, I went a complete blank when I had to choose Why did I pick tweed? You know how it seats.

SUSIE   Well, that depends, if you have a good lining you can —

JACK   Excuse me — you're a Guardian Angel?

ANGEL   I certainly am. (*Looking in her bag.*) I've got a badge somewhere . . .

JACK   (*amused*) And you were at a . . . case conference?

ANGEL   Yes. And if you find it amusing I assure you I do not. We had a sudden influx — deluge — of social workers. Flaunting their degrees — all from polytechnics — and uttering the most dreadful vowel sounds. Since when it's been a nightmare. All they do is set

up workshops in political correctness and
talk about hidden agendas. At the moment
they're trying to negotiate a good behaviour
contract with Rasputin, who's loving the
attention and blaming his mother.

JACK   Rasputin? In heaven?

ANGEL   Rule number 9532861. Never judge a book
            by its cover.

SUSIE   Am I allowed to ask what you do – did?
            When you were . . .

ANGEL   Alive? Ah, I taught stinks and bilge at Saint
            Cedd's. I'd still be there now if I hadn't lost
            my concentration, lit the bunsen burner and –

            (*A phone rings.*)

            Excuse me.

            (*She takes a gold mobile phone from her bag
            and speaks into it.*)

            Yes? . . . What? . . . Where? . . . No, I can't
            I'm in –

            (*She speaks to* JACK.)

            Where am I?

JACK   Err . . . Hampshire.

ANGEL   Thank you. (*Into the mobile.*) Hampshire,
            and there's no way I can get to Glamorgan
            tonight. I'll hit the rush hour . . . What's the
            problem? . . . Oh, send that girl with purple
            hair and the ring in her navel. She thrives on
            domestic violence.

(*She puts the mobile phone away.*)

Go here, go there, never a please or thank
you. That's told them.

JACK   Rush hour? No feathery clouds and shafts of
              sunlight.

ANGEL   Once upon a time, yes. Pleasant float down
              and maybe wave to the odd angel on the
              way. These days – well, if I hadn't grabbed
              onto a meteor I'd still be up there. Now, you
              called me down so what do you want? Quick
              as you can, dear.

SUSIE   (*hesitantly*) I'm awfully sorry but actually I
              called you down for fun.

ANGEL   (*outraged*) Fun? Fun? My in-tray's
              overflowing, my pending file is bursting at
              the seams and you call me down for fun?
              Oh, really, I must get to Glamorgan.

              (*She gets her mobile phone out of the bag.*)

SUSIE   Oh please! I know it was silly of me –

ANGEL   (*tapping in a number*) Very silly. Remember
              the boy who cried wolf?

SUSIE   But since I called you there's been a bit of
              an emergency and –

ANGEL   (*in mid-tap*) Emergency?

SUSIE   Yes, you see what's happened – the young
              couple who live here – she's trying to write
              a book and he's expecting a baby – no, other
              way round. And his mother – no, sorry, –
              her mother is being absolutely –

ANGEL   (*raising a silencing hand*) Please!

                        (*She replaces the phone, puts a hand
                        to either side of her head and makes a
                        humming noise.*)

SUSIE   What's she doing?

JACK   Clearing her sinuses? How do I know. Susie,
                        I don't know which heavenly funny farm
                        she's from but –

ANGEL   So – Flic, Simon, Marcia. All having tea.
                        Right?

SUSIE   (*awed*) Yes . . .

ANGEL   Whole heap of tension, Simon needs to write
                        a successful book or he's going to murder
                        Marcia.

JACK   Oh, I don't think he'll go that far.

ANGEL   Yes, he will. He throws his laptop at her, she
                        falls backwards, hits her head on the hearth.
                        Bingo! He gets twelve years for involuntary
                        manslaughter. Flic – she has a girl, by the
                        way, seven pounds eight ounces – Flic
                        divorces him and marries a complete nerd
                        called William who has an affair with a lap
                        dancer and abandons her.

SUSIE   Wow.

ANGEL   So! This book must be a best seller.

SUSIE   Is there anything you can do?

ANGEL   Nothing at all.

SUSIE   Oh –

ANGEL   But he can. (*To* JACK.) I'm giving you this
            one.

SUSIE   See! I was right. You can creep in here at
            night and –

ANGEL   Whoa, whoa, whoa – Simon's going to write
            it himself but you –

            (*She points at* JACK.)

            – you are going to inspire him.

JACK   Is *how* too silly a question?

ANGEL   Put your hands on my head.

SUSIE   Won't they . . . sink right through?

ANGEL   No, dear, I'm reinforced, (*To* JACK.) Go on!

            (*She sits in the armchair and removes
            her hat.* JACK *goes behind her and very
            reluctantly puts his hands on her head.*)

ANGEL   Good. Now – think of a plot.

JACK   I can't think of a plot just like that!

ANGEL   Oh, for goodness sake – think of a nursery
            rhyme then.

JACK   This is ridiculous.

            (*He closes his eyes.*)

ANGEL   Three blind mice.

JACK   Simple Simon.

ANGEL   There's something wrong here. Try again.

JACK   Oh really . . .

ANGEL   (*after hard concentration*) Little Bo Peep.

JACK   Old Mother Hubbard.

ANGEL   Hang on . . . You're not – (*She shudders.*) –
                an atheist, are you?

JACK   (*smugly*) Card carrying member.

ANGEL   That's it, then. Waste of time. I'll say in my
                report that we –

                (*She starts to rise.*)

SUSIE   Wait – let me.

                (*The* ANGEL *sits and* SUSIE *puts her hands
                on the* ANGEL'S *head, closes her eyes and
                concentrates.*)

ANGEL   Who killed Cock Robin.

SUSIE   Yes! Again.

                (*She closes her eyes and concentrates.*)

ANGEL   Goosey Goosey Gander.

SUSIE   Brilliant.

ANGEL   Right then. Problem solved. (*To* JACK.)
                Doubting Thomas here can tell you what to
                tell him and Bob's your Uncle.

(*She plops her hat on her head, rises and goes to the French windows.*)

SUSIE   Oh, that's wonderful. Thank you so much.

JACK   Just a minute. What do I 'tell her to tell him?' You may arrive out of the blue but plots don't. And I haven't got one.

ANGEL   Yes, you have.

JACK   No, I haven't.

ANGEL   Have.

JACK   Haven't.

ANGEL   Naughty, naughty! What about the one you were about to write when you went for the early bath.

JACK   (*childishly*) That's my plot. Why should I give it to him?

ANGEL   (*with great meaning*) Because, my dear, it's of no earthly use to you.

           (*She smiles, goes to the French windows and exits.*)

SUSIE   Surely you believe now?

JACK   No.

SUSIE   What?

JACK   Gold mobile phones, meteors, case conferences, she's off her trolley. There are men in white coats up there looking for her.

She was floating in the ether and touched
down here.

SUSIE   What you're really saying is you're too
             bloody minded to back down.

JACK   What I'm really saying is one crackpot so
             called angel doth not a heaven make. She
             blew herself up, for God's sake! Probably
             took the whole of the lower fifth with her.

SUSIE   Okay! How did she know what I was
             thinking?

JACK   Because women always know what another
             woman is thinking!

             (SIMON *enters right he crosses to the French*
             windows. Closes them. Grumbling to
             himself.)

SUSIE   So you don't think it's going to work? Well,
             let's find out.

JACK   Why not? I could do with a laugh.

             (SIMON *bends to close the bolt on the*
             windows SUSIE *puts her hands on his head.*)

SIMON   How can she possibly feel a draught through
             all those – Little Jack Horner sat in the
             corner eating his Christmas pie. He put in
             his thumb and took out a plum and said what
             a good boy am I – widow's weeds.

             (*With her hands on* SIMON's *head* SUSIE
             smiles at an amazed JACK.)

             (*End of Act One.*)

ACT TWO

Scene One

The sitting room at Cobbler's Cottage. Three months later.
JACK *and* SIMON *are on the sofa.* JACK *impatiently drumming
his fingers on the arm.* SIMON *reading a book. The French
windows are open. The laptop on the desk.* FLIC, *now six
months pregnant, enters right followed by* SUSIE.

JACK / SIMON	Where have you been?
SUSIE / FLIC	Upstairs. Why?
JACK / SIMON	What were you doing upstairs?
SUSIE / FLIC	Looking at baby clothes.
JACK / SIMON	Again?
FLIC	I thought you were working?
SIMON	I was. I got stuck.
FLIC	Every time I leave the room you get stuck.
JACK	No, every time she leaves the room he gets stuck.
FLIC	Would a cup of coffee help?
SIMON	Please.
	(FLIC *exits right.*)
SUSIE	(*to* SIMON) Selfish pig. You treat her like a slave. (*To* JACK.) I love it when we go through the baby clothes.

JACK   'We' do not go through them. 'She' goes
                through them. You're living her life, you
                know that don't you?

SUSIE   Why not? I can't live mine. Oh . . . it's just
                so nice having another girl around to –

JACK   To what?

SUSIE   Talk to.

JACK   Talk to?

SUSIE   She can't hear me.

JACK   Back off, Susie. Please.

SUSIE   All right!

                (*She moves right.*)

JACK   Where are you going now?

SUSIE   Nowhere.

                (*She returns.*)

JACK   Your eyelid's twitching again. The kitchen.
                That's where you were going. To have a chat
                while she makes the coffee.

SUSIE   I was not!

                (*She goes to the armchair. Is about to sit.*)

JACK   Don't sit down. Tell him to get back to work.

                (*She looks at him.*)

                What?

SUSIE   Stop ordering me around.

JACK   Excuse me? Who asked her Guardian Angel
             for help? Who was told to tell him what I
             told you?

SUSIE   Isn't it about time he worked on his own?

JACK   Yes. But's he got to a tricky plot point and
             needs some help. Don't stand there, put your
             hands on his head.

SUSIE   Don't shout!

             (*She goes behind the sofa and puts her
             hands on* SIMON'S *head.*)

SUSIE   Get on with it then.

JACK   Err . . .

SIMON   Err . . .

JACK   Don't tell him to say 'Err!'

             (SUSIE *takes her hands from* SIMON'S *head.*)

SUSIE   You said 'Err!'

JACK   That was me being me not me telling you to
             tell him!

SUSIE   I am so fed up with this. You being you,
             you being you telling me to tell him. I am
             seriously thinking of using that return
             ticket.

JACK   Before the baby's born? I don't think so.

             (FLIC *enters right with a cup of coffee.*)

FLIC   (*giving* SIMON *the coffee*) What do you think
                of Ferdinand?

                (*She sits next to him and picks up a book of
                baby names.*)

SIMON   What?

FLIC   Ferdinand. If it's a boy.

SUSIE   How many more times – you are having a
                girl!

SIMON   Ferdinand . . . No. It sounds Portuguese.
                And the other kids would call him Ferdy
                Werdy.

SUSIE   Good point.

FLIC   Roderick then? Roddy for short?

SUSIE   Roddy Poddy? That's worse than Ferdy
                Werdy.

SIMON   I quite like that . . .

SUSIE   Oh, you can't!

JACK   Are we writing a book or naming a baby?
                Get him to the bloody desk.

SUSIE   Please do not swear in front of an unborn
                child.

                (*She puts her hands on* SIMON'S *head.*)

SIMON   I must work.

                (SUSIE *removes her hands.*)

FLIC	I thought you were stuck.
SIMON	I am.

(SUSIE *puts her hands back.*)

I was.

(SIMON *goes to the desk and sits.* SUSIE *goes to sit.*)

JACK	Don't sit down come over here.
SUSIE	Please?
JACK	Please.

(*She goes to the desk.*)

JACK   Will you remind him – sorry, will you
            please remind him – that Eva was in Paris
            on the twenty third and couldn't possibly
            have poisoned Peter. Oh! And there's henna
            shampoo in the bathroom and Bertie's as
            bald as a coot.

(SUSIE *repeats the words to herself then
puts her hands on* SIMON'S *head and
concentrates.* SIMON *stops typing, leans
back. Makes a sound of exasperation.*)

SIMON	Damn . . .
FLIC	What?
SIMON	Eva was in –

(SUSIE *lifts her hands and looks at* JACK.)

JACK   Paris!

SUSIE   You gave me my engagement ring in Paris.

JACK   And you dropped it in the Seine.

SUSIE   We're not lucky with water, are we?

             (*She puts her hands back on* SIMON'S *head.*)

SIMON   – Paris on the twenty-third, so she couldn't
             have poisoned Peter.

             (*She lifts her hands.*)

JACK   Shampoo!

             (SUSIE *puts her hands back.*)

SIMON   And there's henna shampoo in the bathroom
             and Peter –

JACK   Bertie! Bertie, Bertie, Bertie!

SIMON   Bertie! Bertie, Bertie, Bertie!

FLIC   What about Bertie?

SUSIE   Yes, what about Bertie?

JACK   He's as bald as a coot, you imbecile.

SIMON   He's as bald as a coot, you imbecile.

FLIC   Thank you very much. I'm sorry your child
             will be born to an imbecile mother!

             (SUSIE, *still with her hands on* SIMON'S *head,
             looks to* JACK *for help.*)

JACK   I didn't mean you, darling, I was . . .

SIMON   I didn't mean you, darling, I was . . .

JACK   . . . talking to myself.

SIMON   . . . talking to myself.

               (SUSIE *removes her hands and sits next to*
               FLIC.)

FLIC   Suppose Eva left the poison in something
               she knew Peter was going to eat. Or drink.

JACK   Don't be ridiculous.

SIMON   Like what?

FLIC   Well, you stick your finger in the peanut
               butter jar every night.

SUSIE   You used to stick yours in the raspberry jam.

SIMON   I do not.

JACK   I did not.

FLIC   Without fail.

SUSIE   Every night.

SIMON   Brilliant. Thanks.

               (*He starts to type.*)

JACK   Oh well, if he's going to listen to you two I
               shan't bother.

SUSIE   But that makes Eva a suspect, it doesn't
               make her the poisoner.

JACK   I don't want her to be a suspect. I'm rotten
                with suspects.

FLIC   No. Don't let Eva do that.

JACK   Why not?

SIMON   Why not?

FLIC   Because if we have a girl I may want to call
                her Eva.

SUSIE   Oh, I like that.

JACK   (*to* SIMON) Don't listen to her. If you want
                Eva to be a suspect have her as a suspect.

SUSIE   But you said –

JACK   Never mind what I said. Tell him.

SUSIE   I am so bored with this . . .

                (*She goes to* SIMON *and tetchily puts her
                hands on his head. She transmits the words
                and her mood.*)

SIMON   (*tetchily*) If I want Eva to be a suspect I'll
                have her as a suspect.

FLIC   Fine! Have her. Why are you being so
                snappy?

                (SUSIE *looks at* JACK.)

JACK   Because it's his bloody book. Tell him!

SIMON   Because it's my bloody book. Tell him!

FLIC   Tell who?

SIMON	What?
FLIC	You said 'Tell him.' Tell who?
JACK	(*to* SUSIE) I don't know. I'm tired. I'm sorry.
SIMON	I don't know. I'm tired. I'm sorry. And sod this for a game of soldiers.

(SUSIE *takes her hands from* SIMON'S *head.*)

SIMON	I've gone completely blank.
FLIC	Well, you said you were tired.
SIMON	Did I?

(SUSIE *puts her hands back on his head.*)

Oh, yes, so I did . . .

(SUSIE *removes her hands. He rises, stretches, goes to* FLIC. *Sits.*)

JACK	Send him back at once! He can't just wander off.

(*With a furious look at* JACK, SUSIE *puts her hands on* SIMON'S *head.*)

SIMON	(*rising with* SUSIE'S *hands still on his head*) I must get back to work.
FLIC	You only just sat down.
SUSIE	Oh, give him a break, please!
JACK	Oh, all right. Five minutes, then.
SIMON	Oh, all right. Five minutes, then.

(SIMON *sits.* SUSIE *removes her hands.* JACK *sits at the desk and looks at the pile of papers.*)

JACK   Tell him it's time he sent a synopsis and the first three chapters to a publisher.

SUSIE   Sorry, I'm on my break.

FLIC   What are you doing about a publisher?

SUSIE   Reception must be very good tonight.

SIMON   (*looking at the book*) Guy. I like that.

FLIC   I said what are you – Guy? Oh, no.

SUSIE   Oh come on, Guy's a lovely name.

SIMON   What's wrong with Guy?

JACK   And why is Guy a lovely name?

FLIC   A Guy sat next to me at school and cut the end off my pigtail.

SUSIE   It just is.

SIMON   That's a daft reason. Guy. I like it,

JACK   Guy as in Guy Fraser, I suppose?

FLIC   Well, I don't. And I'm the one having the baby.

SUSIE   Oh, not that again . . .

SIMON   Thanks to me you're having the baby.

JACK	Again and again and again. Until you tell me the truth.
FLIC	That's a very chauvinist attitude.
SUSIE	I did not go to bed with Guy Fraser.
SIMON	Is that you or your mother speaking?
JACK	You wanted to though, didn't you?
FLIC	On this occasion both of us.
SUSIE	Yes. All right. Yes.
SIMON	You're beginning to sound like her.
JACK	Wanted to or did?
FLIC	My mother talks a lot of sense.
SUSIE	Didn't but wish I had!
SIMON	You can't talk sense through your bottom.
JACK	How do I know you didn't?
FLIC	Right, that's it.
SUSIE	Right, that's it.
	(SUSIE *goes to the French windows.* FLIC *rises and follows her. At the windows* SUSIE *steps back to let* FLIC *go first.*)
FLIC	Thank you.
	(*She exits but remains in view. Stops.* SUSIE *looks at* JACK. *They freeze.* FLIC *turns and enters.*)

FLIC   There's someone here.

SIMON   Yes. Me. Hello.

FLIC   No, someone else.

SIMON   What are you talking about?

FLIC   I'm not sure, but – I was going out and
                someone or something stood back to let me
                go first.

SIMON   Oh, nice manners.

FLIC   I'm serious.

                (JACK *mimes to* SUSIE *that she should put her
                hands on* SIMON's *head. She does so.* JACK
                stands next to her and whispers in her ear.)

SIMON   Flic, come here.

                (*She hesitates.*)

                Come on. Please.

                (FLIC *sits next to him. He puts an arm round
                her.*)

                Now listen, ever since we moved in you've
                secretly hoped that the place is haunted.

                (*She goes to speak.*)

                Yes, you have. I know you have. And maybe
                secretly wishing for it has –

                (JACK *searches for inspiration. Whispers
                again.*)

– has made you very susceptible to
atmosphere. And because I'm so tired –
which is no excuse at all – I've behaved
appallingly and upset you and I am so, so
sorry. And because you were upset you
imagined someone was here, being as kind
as I should have been. Please – forgive me.

(FLIC *looks at him with an unforgiving face.*)

Please?

FLIC   Oh . . . of course I forgive you. And you're
probably right.

SIMON   I know I'm right. What did Guy Fraser have
that I didn't?

(SUSIE *lifts her hands and looks at* JACK.)

FLIC   Who's Guy Fraser?

SIMON   What?

FLIC   You just said 'what did Guy Fraser have that
I – you – didn't.'

(JACK *signals* SUSIE *to put her hands back.
He whispers into her ear.* SUSIE *is bored and
doesn't listen properly.*)

SIMON   Do you know, I'm so deeply into the cook –
rook – book – that lines, thoughts, ideas, are
always floating in my subconscious. They
just sort of flop – hop – pop out.

(JACK *looks at* SUSIE. *She signifies 'sorry'.
He whispers again. She struggles to
understand him.*)

SIMON   Why don't we have a wander round the
               garden? Smell the noses – roses – and deed
               the fishes – feed the dishes. Fishes.

FLIC   You are doing no more work today. Your
               poor brain is absolutely churning.

JACK   What about my poor brain?

               (FLIC *rises. Offers her hand. He rises. They
               go to the French windows and exit.*)

SUSIE   What fishes? The pond's empty.

JACK   What do you want me to do? Pee in it?

               (*He flops into the armchair.*)

SUSIE   Why all the whispering?

JACK   When she saw you I thought maybe she
               could hear us.

SUSIE   How could she possibly have seen me?

JACK   You've got too close to her. Following her
               round all day like a mother hen.

SUSIE   I worry about her.

JACK   Try worrying about me. I'm exhausted; if I
               was alive I'd go for a check-up. He closes his
               eyes.

               (SUSIE *goes to the drinks.*)

SUSIE   Wouldn't a gin and tonic be nice?

JACK   A gin and tonic . . . Oh, how I would like.

SUSIE	Remember Chicago? Top of the Hancock Tower?
JACK	Double Tanqueray . . . crushed ice.
SUSIE	The lights on Navy Pier . . .
JACK	The row we had.
SUSIE	Did we?
JACK	Absolute scorcher.
SUSIE	What was it about?
JACK	Damned if I know . . .
SUSIE	Can you remember what any of our rows were about?
JACK	Not one . . .
SUSIE	What a waste of life . . .
JACK	Yup.
SUSIE	I spend hours thinking about it.
JACK	Life?
SUSIE	Mm . . . Were we always kind, do you suppose?
JACK	You were. That's why Saint Peter knew your name; I was in the query file.
SUSIE	You weren't!
JACK	Felt like it. No, I was always a mean spirited swine, (*Pause.*) unlike Guy Fraser.

SUSIE   Please don't start again about bloody Guy
               bloody Fraser.

JACK   You did lead him on though, didn't you? You
               know you did.

SUSIE   Only when I wanted your attention. I used to
               get so jealous.

JACK   Jealous? I never once looked at or wanted
               another woman.

SUSIE   Of your work. It was so important to you.

JACK   Never more important than you. Never.

SUSIE   Oh . . . of course I wouldn't have slept with
               him. I wouldn't sleep with any man who
               keeps a silver toothpick in his top pocket.
               And he was a lousy tipper. Used to get a
               calculator out and sit there checking the
               VAT. Unlike you who threw notes on the
               table and said finders keepers. No, you've
               always been the only one for me. (*Pause.*)
               And it's a bit late, but I'm truly truly sorry
               for every time I made you unhappy.

JACK   (*looking at her*) Even when you made me
               unhappy I was happy.

SUSIE   That is the sweetest thing you've ever said
               to me. (*She thinks.*) Why didn't you say it
               when you were alive?

JACK   Didn't want you getting above yourself.

SUSIE   I was thinking last night about our first
               home. The studio apartment. Remember?

JACK	Oh God . . . the people upstairs juggled with tyre jacks.
SUSIE	And the people downstairs played The Who's greatest hits . . .
JACK / SUSIE	Very loudly . . .
JACK	And the bed? Remember the bed?
SUSIE	We had to pull it out of the wall.
JACK	Until the night the wall came with it. (*He thinks.*) I made a good job of that plastering.
SUSIE	Oh . . . isn't it sad that we didn't grow old together, into the golden years . . .
JACK	The golden years of incontinence pads and Stannah stairlifts? I'm glad I went before matron had to tell me who I am. I just wish –
SUSIE	What?
JACK	Wish we could go back to the beginning and start again.
SUSIE	We'd make the same mistakes.
JACK	Still be worth it.
	(*He rises and goes to her.*)
	You have no idea how much I want to hold you in my arms.
SUSIE	And you have no idea how much I want you to. (*Pause.*) Hey! Maybe in heaven people can kiss each other.

JACK   I'm not kissing Charlie Ribblestock.

SUSIE   Want to give it another try?

JACK   You know what'll happen. As soon as our
              lips meet we walk through each other.

SUSIE   Oh come on!

              (*They stand in front of the French windows
              and tentatively move their lips closer. As
              their lips are about to meet* SIMON *and* FLIC
              enter. JACK *and* SUSIE *spring apart.*)

SIMON   All I said was –

FLIC   I know what you said. I heard what you said.
              I do not want to hear it again.

              (FLIC *sits on the sofa and picks up the book
              of baby names.*)

SIMON   You are being so unreasonable.

FLIC   La, la, la, la, la, la.

SIMON   Don't be so childish.

FLIC   La la la la la la.

SIMON   Is this what happened at the pony club when
              you didn't win your rosette? La la la la?

FLIC   I did win. I won them all.

SIMON   Only because the judges were frightened of
              your mother.

FLIC   Why do you always blame my mother for
              everything?

SIMON   Because she indulged you rotten and made
           you the spoilt brat you are now.

FLIC   I will not be cooking supper tonight.

SIMON   Yippee.

FLIC   And tomorrow I'm going to go and stay with
           her.

SIMON   Why wait? Go now!

           (*He sits at the desk and looks unseeingly
           at the laptop.* SUSIE *looks from one to the
           other.*)

SUSIE   Oh, stop it both of you!

JACK   Susie –

SUSIE   I can't help it. Don't they know? Don't they
           realise? Life is so so short. Why waste one
           second of it?

JACK   They have to find that out for themselves.

SUSIE   We didn't.

           (*She kneels in front of* FLIC *speaks directly
           to her.*)

           Listen to me – in ten years, two years, ten
           minutes time you won't remember how this
           stupid row started or what it was about. All
           you're doing is using up precious time when
           you could be doing so many other things.
           Laughing, loving, living. Stop it now. Enjoy
           this moment. Because, my darling, none of
           us know how many moments we have. And
           there will come a day when you bitterly

regret every wasted second. Believe me. I know.

(FLIC *remains still while* SUSIE *speaks. After a pause she looks at* SIMON.)

FLIC   I'm sorry.

(SIMON *rushes to the sofa. They kiss.*)

SUSIE   Did she hear me?

JACK   Huddersfield heard you.

FLIC   I'm sorry. It was all my fault.

SIMON   (*kissing her*) No! It was me, it was me. What does it matter how many legs a spider has?

SUSIE   All that over how many legs a – (*She thinks.*) It's six, isn't it?

JACK   Eight.

SUSIE   No, it isn't. It can't be because –

JACK   Hancock Tower?

SUSIE   Hancock Tower. Let's go and deed the fishes.

(*Curtain.*)

Scene Two

The sitting room at Cobbler's Cottage. A few days before Christmas. Christmas cards on the bookcase and on the small tables. The curtains are closed at the French windows. Right of the windows a partly decorated Christmas tree in a tub. SIMON *is at the laptop.* JACK *is reading over his shoulder.* FLIC *is kneeling on the floor decorating the tree. She has a box of ornaments. The baby is obviously imminent.*

FLIC   (*singing*) Away in a manger, no crib for a
                bed . . . What do you want on the top of the
                tree? Silver star or the angel?

JACK   Silver star.

SIMON   Angel.

                (FLIC *searches in the box. Takes out the
                angel.*)

FLIC   Oh, she's lost her wings . . .

JACK   They all have, love.

FLIC   I'm going to make a wish. She holds the
                angel, closes her eyes, and wishes.

SIMON   What did you wish for?

JACK   Don't –

FLIC   The most perfect baby in the world. (*She
                puts the angel on the top of the tree.*)

JACK   You should never tell a wish . . .

                (*He looks again at what* SIMON *is typing.
                Obviously not happy. He goes to the sofa,
                giving* FLIC *an indulgent smile as he passes.
                He sits.* SUSIE *enters right, she surveys the
                room.*)

SUSIE   Ah . . . isn't this cosy?

(*She goes to* SIMON *and is about to put her hands on his head.*)

JACK   What are you doing?

SUSIE   Telling him to tell Flic her mince pies need to come out.

JACK   Stop interfering. You caused enough trouble yesterday with the spaghetti.

SUSIE   It was boiling dry, she was resting –

FLIC   (*holding up an ornament*) Do you remember when we bought this?

JACK   Stop interfering.

SIMON   (*giving a quick glance at the ornament*) No.

SUSIE   What's wrong?

FLIC   Camden Market? That sweet man with the glass eye.

JACK   Nothing's wrong. And I wish you wouldn't – Didn't we buy some things from him?

SUSIE   Something is wrong because – Who?

SIMON   (*who has been trying to remember*) A man with a glass eye . . .

SUSIE   For days now you've – Do you remember that man with the glass eye in Camden Market?

JACK   (*to himself*) Sometimes I find all this very tiring . . .

FLIC My mince pies! Could you get them out.

SIMON Just a sec.

(SUSIE *puts her hands on his head.*)

Sorry, darling. I'll get them out now.

(SIMON *exits right.* SUSIE *reads what he was typing. Looks at* JACK. *Reads some more.*)

SUSIE (*casually*) Eva's character's changed a lot, hasn't she?

JACK Everyone's changed a lot. The Chief Inspector is now a woman who spends most of her time trying to adopt a Romanian orphan. Bald Bertie is a transvestite with a vocation who can't decide whether to be a monk or a nun, and Peter was poisoned by his six year old daughter who is – wait for it – controlled by an alien power.

SUSIE Wow. Well, when he comes back do you want me to –

JACK It doesn't work anymore. It hasn't worked for weeks. He writes what I tell him then he changes it back.

SUSIE Aha! So that's what's wrong with you.

JACK Oh please. Do you think I'm so small minded that his writing a book without my help would upset me?

SUSIE Yes.

JACK You're right.

(FLIC *rises. Her hand in the small of her*
back. As she goes to sit on the sofa SUSIE
puts a cushion behind her.)

JACK   Do you want her to know you're here?

SUSIE   She does know.

JACK   How do you know she does know?

SUSIE   I just know.

JACK   Yes, but how do you – Why am I arguing
              with Hampton Court Maze?

              (FLIC *looks at the tree. Puts her hands on*
              her stomach.)

FLIC   Next year, little baby, you'll be looking at
              your first Christmas tree. And when you
              wake up on Christmas morning there'll be
              a stocking full of presents. If we have the
              money to buy any . . .

SUSIE   Oh dear . . .

JACK   You know, there are times when I wish she
              had married William.

SUSIE   William? The nerd who sniffs the cork?

JACK   There are worse things than sniffing wine
              corks, Susie, far worse things. Here she
              is – pregnant – living in a rented cottage –
              worried about money. Sorry but . . . I love
              the girl.

SUSIE   So do I. (*Pause.*) Is this how parents feel, do
              you suppose?

JACK	If it is, it hurts. One hell of a lot.

(SIMON *enters right. He carries a plate of mince pies. Offers them to* FLIC.)

FLIC	No thank you, darling. I think I'm going to go and put my feet up.
JACK	Good.
SIMON	You're okay?
FLIC	Fine! Stop worrying. Finish the tree.

(SIMON *helps her up. She exits right.*)

JACK	Aren't you going up to keep an eye on her?
SUSIE	You said not to interfere.
JACK	When have you ever paid any attention to anything I say?

(SUSIE *exits right.* SIMON *goes to the tree. Picks an ornament out of the box. Looks at it. Puts it back.*)

JACK	Oh, make an effort, man!

(*The doorbell rings.* SIMON *exits right.* JACK *rises, goes to the box of ornaments, selects one and is about to put it on the tree when* MARK *enters right. He looks round warily. Looks at the tree.* JACK *decides to have some fun. Takes the ornament and with an eye on* MARK *slowly puts it on the tree.* MARK *sees an ornament travelling through the air and attaching itself to the tree. He stands transfixed. Only his eyes move as he looks round the room.* SIMON *enters right.*)

SIMON   Sit down, Mr Webster.

                 (MARK *doesn't move.*)

                 Mr Webster?

                 (*He touches his arm.* MARK *jumps.*)

                 Why don't you sit down?

                 (MARK *sits in the armchair. His eyes still on
                 the tree.*)

                 Flic's having a rest. Cup of tea? Drink?

MARK   Drink.

SIMON   Right.

                 (*He goes to the drinks.*)

                 Scotch?

MARK   Yes.

SIMON   (*pouring a scotch*) Neat?

MARK   Very.

                 (SIMON *adds more scotch and gives it to*
                 MARK *who drinks it down in one and hands*
                 SIMON *the glass.*)

SIMON   Another?

MARK   Yes. Please.

                 (*Puzzled, but finding the situation amusing,*
                 SIMON *pours another drink and hands it*

to MARK, *who again drinks it down. He*
continues to stare at the tree.)

SIMON   (*with his back to the tree*) Is there a problem
             with the lease?

             (MARK *still stares at the tree.*)

             Mr Webster? Mr Webster?

MARK   (*trying to get to grips*) What?

SIMON   Is there a problem with the lease?

MARK   Lease?

SIMON   Yes, is there a –

             (JACK *drapes a string of tinsel on the tree.*
             MARK *makes a whimpering sound and puts a*
             hand to his cheek.)

SIMON   Are you in pain?

MARK   Pain? Yes. Pain. I am. A tooth.

SIMON   Oh, I'm sorry. I suppose so close to
             Christmas it's difficult to get an –

MARK   Have you . . . have you . . . been happy here,
             Mr Willis?

SIMON   Happy? Yes, very. Why?

MARK   Nothing's happened to . . . worry you?

SIMON   Worry me? No. Why do you ask?

MARK   Because . . . because . . . the thing is –

(JACK *moves the angel from left to right.*
MARK *stares at the tree.*)

SIMON   Yes?

MARK   Sorry?

SIMON   You said 'the thing is.'

MARK   Did I?

               (*He looks at* SIMON.)

               Oh. Yes. Mrs Cameron's niece in Australia,
               she . . . she . . .

               (*He looks back at the tree.* SIMON *follows his
               gaze. Sees nothing but the tree. Looks back
               at* MARK.)

               She . . . she's selling the cottage.

JACK   (*in an Aussie accent*) Nowhere to put the
               barbie.

SIMON   Does that mean we've got to move? Because
               the baby's due any day and I don't fancy
               tramping round looking for a stable.

MARK   Sorry?

               (*He looks at* SIMON *then back at the tree.*)

               Oh . . . stable . . . yes . . . no . . .

SIMON   Mr Webster, is there something wrong?
               Besides your tooth?

MARK   Tooth? Oh, tooth. Nothing. Nothing.
               Absolutely nothing.

(SUSIE *enters right.*)

SUSIE   I thought I recognised the aftershave.

MARK   (*desperately pulling himself together*)
        Webster, Webster and Webster were
        wondering whether you were interested in
        putting in an offer.

        (SUSIE *looks at* JACK.)

JACK   Brenda's selling.

SUSIE   No!

SIMON   An offer? You mean buy Cobbler's Cottage?
        Wow . . .

JACK   I think you mean 'how?'

SUSIE   We should have left it to them.

JACK   Yes . . . (*Realising.*) We didn't know them!

SIMON   There's nothing we'd like more, Mr Webster,
        but it's a bit beyond us at the moment.
        Perhaps you could give us a little time to
        think about it?

        (MARK *is staring at the tree.*)

        Could you?

MARK   Sorry?

SIMON   Could you give us a little time?

MARK   Time?

SIMON   To think about it?

SUSIE   What's wrong with him?

JACK   I'll show you in a minute.

                    (*The doorbell rings.*)

JACK   This is ridiculous! The girl's trying to rest.

SIMON   Excuse me a moment.

                    (SIMON *exits right.* MARK *again stares at the tree.*)

JACK   Watch this.

                    (*He goes to the tree and moves the angel from side to side.* MARK *is again transfixed.*)

SUSIE   Hey!

                    (*She goes to the tree and takes an ornament.* MARK *makes small noises of fear.*)

MARK   Is there anybody there?

                    (SUSIE *describes a circle with the ornament.*)

                    Is that you. Jack Cameron?

                    (SUSIE *walks towards* MARK *holding the ornament in front of her. When she reaches* MARK *he leans back as far as he can. She puts it in his top pocket. He waits a moment then with his right hand he takes it very warily from his pocket and looks at it as if expecting it to explode. He is staring at it as* MARCIA *enters right followed by* SIMON.)

SIMON   Marcia, this is Mark Webster, the estate
                    agent who looks after Cobbler's Cottage,

(*To* MARK.) This is Marcia Bradshaw. Flic's mother.

MARCIA (*extending a hand*) How do you do, Mr Webster?

 (MARK *rises to shake her hand. Realises he is holding the ornament. Puts it in his pocket. Shakes hands. Sits.*)

JACK I am doing this on behalf of the gazumped . . .

SIMON Do sit down, Marcia.

 (MARCIA *sits on the sofa.* MARK *stares at the tree.*)

SIMON Would you like a drink?

MARK Yes.

MARCIA (*giving* MARK *a chilling glance*) No, thank you.

SIMON Same again, Mr Webster?

MARK What?

SIMON Another scotch?

MARK Yes.

 (SIMON *pours him a scotch.*)

JACK That's his third.

MARCIA So Felicity is resting?

SUSIE (*answering* JACK) No?

SIMON   Yes.

                (*He gives* MARK *his drink.* MARK *drinks it
                straight down.*)

MARCIA   And she's still insisting on having the baby
                here?

SIMON   Absolutely. Everything's set up. And there
                haven't been any problems.

JACK   She should go to hospital.

MARCIA   She should go to hospital. First babies can
                be tricky.

JACK   Exactly.

SIMON   In which case we would call an ambulance.

MARCIA   Which will have great difficulty negotiating
                the cart track.

JACK   She's got a point there.

MARCIA   As you refused my invitation for Christmas
                Day I've brought you a hamper of delicacies.

SIMON   That's very kind of you.

MARCIA   No. It's very practical. I couldn't see how
                you could afford luxury items.

SUSIE   Oh, don't shame him in front of an estate
                agent.

SIMON   Well, thanks very much. I'll just get it out of
                the car then. (*He speaks to* MARK.) Shan't be
                a second.

(*He exits right.*)

MARCIA   Tell me, Mr Webster, is it septic tank or
              main drainage?

MARK   (*his eyes on the tree*) Pardon?

MARCIA   The cottage. Septic tank or main drainage?
              Because I can definitely detect a whiff.

MARK   A what?

MARCIA   A whiff.

MARK   A whiff of what?

MARCIA   Septic tank.

MARK   Septic tank?

MARCIA   So is it?

MARK   Is it what?

MARCIA   Septic tank?

MARK   I have no idea . . .

MARCIA   Why are you staring at that tree?

MARK   What? Oh, because it's – it's – it's . . . very
              pretty.

              (*He looks at* MARCIA. *Smiles weakly.*)

MARCIA   So what brings you here, Mr Webster? Not
              unpaid rent, I hope.

JACK   You wish.

MARK   I . . . I wanted to tell Mr Willis that the
              cottage is going on the market.

MARCIA   Really? Well, I suppose if it were completely
              gutted . . .

JACK   Gutted? It's not a herring!

MARCIA   And extended. It's . . . pathetically small . . .

SUSIE   That does it. That bloody does it.

MARCIA   Only one bathroom and –

              (SUSIE *puts her hands on* MARCIA's *head.*)

              – You have very sensual lips, Mr Webster.

              (MARK *stares at her.* SUSIE *lifts her hands.*)

              – no fitted cupboards –

              (SUSIE *replaces her hands.*)

              – I want you to press them on mine.

              (SUSIE *removes her hands.*)

              – a lean-to kitchen –

              (SUSIE *replaces her hands.*)

              Three years is a long time, Mr Webster.

MARK   I beg your pardon?

MARCIA   Three years without passion, without love,
              without a man's hands on my yearning
              body . . .

JACK   Steady!

MARK   (*looking at his watch*) Is that the time?

MARCIA   Yes! Yes! Yes! Yes! It is the time. The time
                is now. Now, Mr Webster. Take me. Take
                me!

MARK   Take you where?

MARCIA   Take me here. Daddy will understand. My
                body craves fulfilment.

                (*With* SUSIE'S *hands still on her head she
                rises and advances towards* MARK.)

JACK   Stop now. Before she strips down to her
                corsets.

SUSIE   Oh . . .

                (SUSIE *removes her hands.* MARCIA *still
                advances. She hitches up her skirt, pushes*
                MARK *back in the chair and sits astride
                him. He puts his arms down by his sides and
                leans far back.* JACK *and* SUSIE *are thrilled.*)

MARK   Madam, I am a married man!

MARCIA   I don't care!

                (*She takes his face in her hands and kisses
                him.*)

                Let us strip naked and writhe upon the rug!

                (*She kisses him again.*)

JACK   What is she on?

SUSIE   Him!

MARCIA   Don't fight it, Mr Webster! Kiss me, kiss me.

                (SIMON *enters right.*)

SIMON   I've put the hamper in the . . .

                (*He stops dead. Unable to believe his eyes.*)

                Marcia!

                (MARCIA *stops kissing* MARK. *Sees* SIMON. *Realises the position she is in.*)

MARCIA   What happened?

MARK   Nothing! I assure you, Madam, nothing!

SUSIE   Members of the jury . . .

SIMON   I didn't realise you . . . knew each other?

MARK / MARCIA   We don't.

JACK   You do now.

                (MARCIA *rises. Pulls her skirt down.*)

SIMON   Well, I'm glad you've . . . got acquainted.

MARCIA   How did that happen?

MARK   Madam, I have no idea. Mr Willis, I do assure, you must believe me, what you saw was . . . was . . . nothing to do with me!

SIMON   You have had three large whiskeys.

MARK   Had I had three dozen large whiskeys I
              would never never have . . .

              (*He looks at* MARCIA.)

              I must go. I really must go.

              (*He rises and stands not quite knowing how
              to leave. Decides upon convention.*)

              Goodbye, Mrs Bradshaw.

MARCIA   Goodbye, Mr Webster.

              (*Skirting* MARCIA, MARK *moves right. He
              stops. Looks at the tree.* JACK *moves the
              angel.* MARK *makes a whimpering sound
              then exits right. There is a pause.* MARCIA
              *goes to the drinks. Pours a scotch. Drinks it
              down in one.*)

JACK   That's not the first time she's done that.

MARCIA   I would prefer it if Felicity didn't know that
              I was . . .

SIMON   (*blank faced*) Unwell?

MARCIA   Yes.

SIMON   Of course.

MARCIA   Thank you. I think I had better go home
              and . . .

SIMON   Rest?

MARCIA   Rest, Yes.

SIMON   You do look a little tired.

(MARCIA *moves right.*)

SIMON   Oh – thanks for the hamper!

MARCIA   Hamper? Oh, hamper. Yes.

                 (*She looks again at the chair. Then exits
                 right.* SIMON *at last lets go and starts to
                 laugh.*)

SIMON   Kiss me, kiss me!

JACK   Take me, take me!

SUSIE   Let us strip naked and writhe upon the rug!

                 (*All three are laughing helplessly as* FLIC
                 enters right.)

FLIC   What's so funny?

SIMON   What? Oh, that . . . (*He tries to control
                 himself.*) It's just that . . .

JACK   Oh, tell her!

SIMON   Your mother. She – she –

                 (*He starts to laugh again.*)

FLIC   She what?

SIMON   She – she – brought a hamper round. And –
                 and –

FLIC   And what?

SUSIE   She's going to hit him in a minute.

SIMON   (*wiping his eyes*) And nothing. She – she –

FLIC	Something must have happened. Did she take all her clothes off and do a war dance on the rug?

JACK	Close. Very close.

(SIMON *is again hysterical.* FLIC *looks at him with extreme annoyance.*)

FLIC	I'm going back upstairs; if you ever recover I'd like a cup of –

(*She gasps and puts her arms across her stomach.* SIMON *instantly stops laughing.*)

SIMON	What?

FLIC	I don't know.

(*She gasps again.*)

FLIC	Oh . . . I think . . . maybe I'm having the baby.

(*Curtain.*)

Scene Three

Early hours of the morning of the next day. The sitting room at Cobbler's Cottage. JACK *is pacing the floor.* SUSIE *enters right* JACK *looks at her. She shakes her head. Sits and adds ornaments to the tree.*

JACK	What are you doing?

SUSIE	Finishing the tree.

JACK	Shouldn't you be up there?

SUSIE	Doing what? I keep getting in the way.

JACK   How can a ghost get in the way?

SUSIE   It's a small bedroom, Simon's next to the
                bed, the nurse – a large lady – is here, there
                and everywhere. She's walked through me
                twice.

                (JACK *goes to the door right.*)

SUSIE   Where are you going?

JACK   (*nobly*) One of us should be up there.

SUSIE   If the one of us is you – not a good idea.

JACK   I'm not going to faint, am I?

                (*He exits right.* SUSIE *looks after him.*
                Shakes her head. Adds an ornament to the
                tree. SIMON *enters right. Goes straight to*
                the drinks. Pours a scotch. Drinks it down.
                A pole-axed JACK *enters right. Looks at*
                SIMON.)

JACK   You. Straight after Christmas. Vasectomy.

                (SIMON *exits right.* JACK *collapses onto the*
                sofa.)

SUSIE   I did warn you.

JACK   Why do women go through all that? It's . . .
                it's . . . it's –

SUSIE   Wonderful when it's all over. Or so I've
                heard.

JACK   That nurse woman is totally incompetent.

SUSIE   Is she? When I was up there she seemed to
         know what she was doing.

JACK   Then why did she bring her knitting?

SUSIE   Because it could be a long wait. First babies
         can take a time.

JACK   How much time? It's been eleven hours!

SUSIE   Which is nothing for a first baby.

JACK   How do you know?

SUSIE   The nurse said.

JACK   The nurse said. She should have a team of
         top consultants. Not a soothsayer in a pinny
         with a ball of Kwik Knit.

         (*He watches her decorate the tree.*)

JACK   I'm glad we never had a child. Oh, I can't
         bear to think of it.

SUSIE   Me suffering, you mean.

JACK   Mm? Oh, no. It being an orphan.

SUSIE   On which happy note –

         (*She rises.*)

         – I'm going back up. If the nurse is knitting
         there should be room for me.

         (*She goes to the door right.* JACK *senses a
         slight frostiness.*)

JACK   What's the matter? What have I done?

SUSIE   Think about it.

             (*She exits right.* JACK *rises. Walks around,
             his lips moving as he goes through their
             recent conversation. Light dawns.*)

JACK   Good God, do I have to watch every little P
             and every little Q?

             (SUSIE *enters right.*)

             Look, you know what I meant –

SUSIE   (*wildly excited*) It's happening. It's all
             happening. Any minute now. I can see the
             head!

JACK   Whose head?

SUSIE   The baby's head!

JACK   Oh. (*He thinks.*) If you can see the head why
             can't you see the – Oh! Get back up there.
             Don't worry about me, I'll be all right.

SUSIE   Oh, good.

             (*She exits right.* JACK *goes to the tree and
             looks at the angel.*)

JACK   A perfect baby? Remember? Just make sure
             she gets her wish.

             (*He looks more closely.*)

             You're cross-eyed, do you know that? No
             wings and cross-eyed. Some angel you are.

             (*He goes to the French windows. Pulls back
             a curtain. Looks out. Speaks to the angel.*)

It's snowing. Great curling flakes like goose
feathers. I haven't seen flakes like that
since I was a little boy. I was in bed with
the eiderdown under my chin – What was
wrong with me? Chicken Pox? (*He thinks
for a moment.*) Anyway, I could see through
the window these huge great – Oh, my God.
Snow. If they need an ambulance they'll
never get up the track. Damn, damn, damn,
I knew she should have gone to hospital.
William would have insisted she went to
hospital. He'd probably have a lap dancer
round for the night but –

(*He has a sudden thought.*)

They could land a helicopter in the field. Yes.

(SUSIE *enters right. Stands in the doorway.*)

It's snowing but it's all right, they can land
a – What? What is it?

SUSIE   It's a girl. The nurse is frantic. She isn't
            breathing.

JACK   Silly cow. Wallop her on the back.

SUSIE   The baby! The baby isn't breathing. The
            nurse is trying everything. Oh, Jack, she's
            so beautiful. And Flic was so brave.

            (SUSIE *exits right.* JACK *is distraught. He
            paces back and forth.*)

JACK   Come on, little baby, come on.

            (*He paces some more. Thinking deeply.
            Agonises. Decides.*)

Okay, okay, this is – hang on. Let's go the
whole hog.

(*He puts his hands together in prayer.*)

Okay. This is me. Jack Cameron. Atheist.
Asking you – begging you – to please please
please help that baby. Take it out on me, not
her. Purgatory. Hellfire. Throw the book at
me. Anything. It doesn't matter. Just make
that baby breathe. (*Pause.*) Look, I'm sorry
for every rotten thing I've ever done and
every rotten thing I've ever said and I'm
sorry I said you don't exist, (*Pause.*) but if
I really believed it I wouldn't be talking to
you now, would I? (*Pause.*) I'm praying, for
God's sake, what more do you want? Have a
heart. One little baby . . . Wait a minute.

(*He gets down on his knees.*)

Does that help?

(*He waits. After a moment he starts to rise.
There is the sound of a baby crying. He gets
down again.*)

Oh . . . Thank you. Thank you so much . . .
Look, there probably isn't but if there's ever
anything I can do for you, you only have to
say.

(*The* ANGEL *enters right. Dressed as before
and with her capacious bag.*)

ANGEL   There's a sight for sore eyes.

(JACK *looks at her, astounded.*)

JACK   I didn't call you.

ANGEL   Yes, you did.

JACK   No, I didn't.

ANGEL   Did.

JACK   Didn't.

             (SUSIE *enters right.*)

SUSIE   Oh, Jack, it was a miracle. She –

             (*She sees the* ANGEL.)

             I didn't call you.

ANGEL   We've done all that, dear.

JACK   Apparently I did.

SUSIE   How? You don't believe in –

             (*She realises he is on his knees.*)

             You didn't?

ANGEL   He did.

JACK   (*rising*) I did a bit.

SUSIE   You prayed? You actually prayed?

JACK   It was all I could think of . . .

ANGEL   He made a good job of it, too. Enough for
             me to get an SOS call. Top priority. And that
             doesn't happen very often, I can tell you.

SUSIE   (*awed*) Jack Cameron prayed . . .

ANGEL   Don't go on about it, dear. Right. Lickety
                 spit. Let's get going. It's very lucky his
                 return ticket hasn't expired.

JACK   Going?

ANGEL   Yes, going. Surely you realised when you
                 prayed that you couldn't stay here.

JACK   Oh come on! I mean I just sort of got down
                 on my knees and – she might have breathed
                 anyway!

ANGEL   Don't split hairs. You prayed. You go.

                 (*Her mobile phone rings. She gets it from
                 the bag and answers it.*)

                 Yes? . . . I know we should. Slight hitch. Tell
                 him I'm sorry.

                 (*She puts the phone away.*)

                 He who must be obeyed has spoken.

SUSIE   But that's not fair.

ANGEL   The times I hear that . . .

SUSIE   Not that we've got to go. It's the baby. I
                 want to know about the baby.

JACK   And his book? What about his book?

ANGEL   (*sighing deeply*) All right, all right! I'll see
                 if I can get through but in this weather . . .

                 (*She puts a hand to either side of her head
                 and makes a humming noise. She shakes her
                 head.*)

ANGEL	No good. I'll have to change frequencies.
	(*She adjusts her humming to a higher pitch.* JACK *looks pained.*)
JACK	She'll break a wine glass in a minute.
ANGEL	That's more like it. Right. Susie has a –
SUSIE	They call her Susie . . .
ANGEL	Susie has a wonderful life. Gets physics degree, marries a vet, has three children. The book – I shouldn't be telling you any of this – the book is a bestseller.
JACK	They can buy the cottage.
ANGEL	They can buy Hampshire. He sells the film rights.
JACK	Who plays Eva?
ANGEL	I'm a Guardian Angel, not a casting director. Now, if you're ready.
	(JACK *moves to the door right.*)
	Where are you going?
JACK	To see the baby.
ANGEL	Then see her. He looks at her blankly. Close your eyes and concentrate. Get on with it!
	(JACK *closes his eyes.*)
SUSIE	No one told us we could do that!

ANGEL   Really? They should have done. File a
            complaint when you get up there.

JACK   Oh . . . she is so gorgeous . . .

SUSIE   Do you . . . do you think Flic knew that I
            was here.

ANGEL   Oh yes. One can always sense love.

JACK   I think she's got my hands.

            (SUSIE *looks at* JACK *standing with his eyes
            closed.*)

SUSIE   He's so sweet.

ANGEL   (*doubtfully*) Yes . . .

SUSIE   Can we . . . can we touch each other? Up
            there?

ANGEL   I've said too much already.

SUSIE   Well, just in case we can't. Could we possibly
            . . . I mean do you think we could . . .

            (*She looks pleadingly at the* ANGEL.)

ANGEL   You are pushing your luck.

SUSIE   Please? He did pray.

ANGEL   Oh . . . very well. But be quick. No long
            lingerings.

SUSIE   Thank you.

(*She puts her arms round* JACK *who still has his eyes closed. He opens them and kisses her. He looks at the* ANGEL.)

JACK   I suppose we couldn't . . .

ANGEL   No. You definitely couldn't. Ready?

SUSIE   Yes. No!

              (*She closes her eyes. Smiles as she sees the baby.*)

              Goodbye my love, have such a happy life.

              (*She opens her eyes.*)

              Sorry about that. Yes. Ready.

              (SUSIE *and* JACK *look round the room and then at each other.*)

JACK   All that pearly gate bit again.

ANGEL   No, straight in this time. They've done the paperwork.

SUSIE   Oh well, that's something.

JACK   Still a bit scary.

SUSIE   Not as scary as drowning.

JACK   True. And we survived that.

              (*They realise how funny this is and laugh.*)

ANGEL   Do you want to get me downgraded? We have to go!

SUSIE   Do we . . . close our eyes?

ANGEL   Up to you. (*She smiles at them.*) Pity to miss
               the stars.

               (*They stand completely still. Stage lights up
               to maximum. Blackout. Curtain.*)

               The end.